THE FIRST OLYMPIC GAMES

Barbara Christesen

Illustrated by
Lynn Sweat

cpi
contemporary perspectives, inc.

This book is distributed by Silver Burdett Company, Morristown, New
Jersey, 07960.

Library of Congress Number: 78-15976

Cover illustration by Lynn Sweat
Every effort has been made to trace the ownership of all copyrighted
material in this book and to obtain permission for its use.

Library of Congress Cataloging in Publication Data

Christesen, Barbara, 1940-
  The first Olympic games.
  SUMMARY: A description of the ancient Olympic games, as
seen through the eyes of a young Greek boy, is accompanied by
a history of the games from ancient times to the present.
  1. Olympic games (Ancient) — Juvenile literature.
[1. Olympic games — History] I. Title
GV23.C46   796.4'8   78-15976
ISBN 0-89547-043-8

Manufactured in the United States of America
ISBN 0-89547-043-8

Contents

THE FIRST OLYMPICS

Had you been watching us from Mount Olympus that day more than 2,500 years ago you might have heard the roar of the crowd. Even this far away you could have seen the thousands of people jammed into the valley. You might have just made out the young men straining their bodies to reach the finish line first.

The sudden burst of noise would have filled you with wonder. "What is happening down there?" you would have asked. How could you know that in that valley the lifelong dream of a young man, his father, and a whole city had just come true? "But it only looked like a race," you might say. *Only* a race! My friend, that was not just any race. That was an *Olympic* race.

I saw that race. I am Pindar and it was my lifelong dream that had come true. It was the last of the year's Olympic games and my son, Diagoras, had won. But he did not just win the race. Diagoras won the *Pentathlon* — the greatest of all Olympic games! For the past four years, since the last Olympic games were played, my son was training for that moment. Diagoras became the champion of the Olympics — the champion of all Greece.

When Diagoras won, he felt as if he were dreaming. He walked up to the judges to get the greatest prize of all in Greece — the branch of olive leaves. I have never been so proud. Now the whole country would know my son, Diagoras — the hero.

When Diagoras and I went home to Arcadia, everyone in the city was waiting for us. The men carried Diagoras through the city gate on their shoulders. We paraded through the streets. Poets had already written songs about my son and all through the city people were singing them. Along the way we saw statues of Diagoras. The statues made him look almost like a god, strong and handsome.

As I listened to the cheers of the crowd, I thought back to the first time I told Diagoras of the Olympics and what the games meant to Greece. It was just six years ago this day. Diagoras was little more than 11 years old.

Chapter 1

Diagoras Hears About the Olympics

From the time he was old enough to play with other children, Diagoras loved sports. He would try *anything* — running, jumping, wrestling — all the games that the boys of our city liked to play. What is more, he was good at every game he tried. Everyone in Arcadia said so. They *had* to. There was not a boy in town who could beat Diagoras at anything.

One day I watched Diagoras running a race against four other boys. No sooner had he beat them when each of the boys took a turn wrestling with Diagoras. One by one he pinned each of them. And he was not even tired! He wanted to stay and play more games. But it was time to go home for dinner.

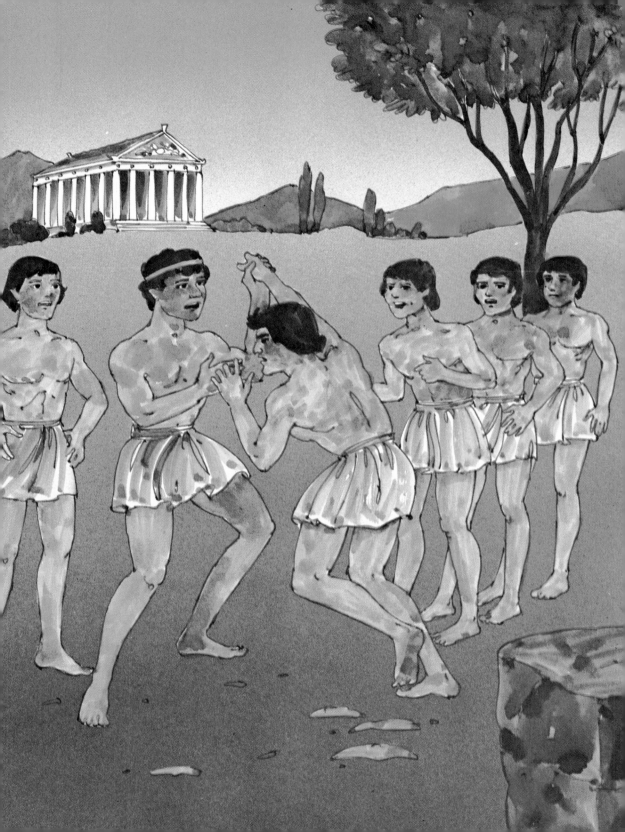

As we walked home I found myself saying things to Diagoras I thought I would not say for many years. "My boy, you are a born athlete. When you grow up you will be good enough to enter the Olympic games. And you will *win*. I have the feeling you will make your family and all of Arcadia very proud of you."

Diagoras could not really be sure about what I was telling him. He was still so young. Oh, he had heard of the Olympic games of course. Was there anyone in all the land who did not know the ancient Greek games? But he did not yet understand what they were. He could not yet know how important the Olympics were to his people — we who lived in the land where the Olympic games were born.

"I want to make you proud of me, Papa," Diagoras said to me. "But tell me. Why are the Olympic games more important than any other games? And why would all of Arcadia be proud of me if I won them?"

I remember smiling down at him when he asked about the Olympic games. How could I tell this boy, still so young, that the Olympics were the very life of Greece? Could I make him understand that, without the games, there would be no Greece as we knew it? I would try. And so I began to tell Diagoras the story of the first Olympic games.

Chapter 2

How the
Olympics Began

Sports had always been very important to the people of ancient Greece. Games were played when people married, when they died, and on all holidays. We knew that the gods were very pleased with anyone who proved to be a fine athlete. We believed that Zeus, the strongest of all the gods, was most happy when games were held in his name.

Our country was really like a group of smaller countries. Each was called a *city-state* because the people who lived there often felt their city was different from all other parts of the country. People who lived in the city of Corinth called themselves Corinthians, not Greeks. People from Arcadia called themselves Arcadians, and so on.

More than 200 years before Diagoras was born, the city-states of Elis and Pisa were at war with each other. It was a foolish war, as most wars are, that started late in the spring. Soon the hot summer came. Food had to be grown. And after that there were grapes and olives to be picked. But all the men were off fighting a war. Their familes would not be able to take care of the crops alone.

At last, in the summer of 776 B. C., the leaders of Elis and Pisa agreed to end the fighting. There was joy in both cities. The people planned games for the gods. Their athletes would show the gods how thankful they were for the end of the war. Each city chose to have its games in the valley of Olympia where the god Zeus and his wife Hera lived in great temples.

What a strange time it must have been in Olympia. People from Elis and Pisa, who hated one another only a few days before, came together to worship their gods. Now it seemed foolish that each city-state should

plan its own games. Perhaps only *one* great festival should be held. People from both cities would take part in it.

By the August full moon the crops would be picked. That was when the games would be held. And they would take place right here in the valley of Olympia in the shadow of the great temples. For this was special ground. It had always been kept apart for religious worship. War was never fought on this land. Everyone would feel safe here — as brothers should feel safe with one another.

And so Elis played Pisa in the world's first Olympic games. At least these games are the first about which anyone knows, or about which any writing has ever been found. The first Olympics lasted only one day. Only running contests were held. A man named Coroebus was the winner of the first Olympic race. But no one knows how fast or how far he ran. Such things were never important in the ancient Olympic games. *Winning was all that mattered.*

Over the years the Olympics grew from one day to a week. Many other games were added. Wrestling, jumping, boxing, throwing, horse racing, and chariot racing were made part of the Olympic contests. Each city-state sent its best athletes to Olympia every four years. There they competed to win in honor of Zeus. They became prouder of Olympic honors than of winning wars.

The greatest honor that could be given to any Greek was to win the branch of olive leaves. It was the only prize given to the winner of an Olympic game. Kings entered the games along with the rest of the people. They all wanted the honor of being crowned with the olive branch — a sign of peace.

The Olympic games were open to all Greek men who were known to be good and fair persons. Women, foreigners, slaves, and anyone in disgrace for any reason were all kept out of the games. Women could not even watch the games!

That was all I had time to tell Diagoras that afternoon. But it was enough. He began to understand why the Olympics were so important. I knew he understood because of one more question he asked just before he went to bed that night. "Father," he asked, "will people ever have to fight wars again when they have the Olympic games instead?"

Chapter 3

A Trip to Olympia

It was my son's 13th birthday. I had been planning a gift for him for some time. Now I would let him know about it. I called him in from the fields where he was working. He knew it must be something important.

"This is the year of the Olympic games," I told my son. "Diagoras, I think you are old enough to understand them. So in August you and I will go to Olympia together."

Diagoras was so excited he could not speak at first. His lips moved, his eyes were wide, but he did not seem to find a voice. I laughed at him, but I knew how happy my gift had made him. From that moment, he made a scratch on some stone for every day that passed until the August full moon.

I tell you that boy worked twice as fast as ever in the fields. I never saw anyone try so hard from early morning to late at night. And when the crops were in, I kept my word. Diagoras and I left for Olympia.

We travelled for many days on foot. We carried our food and a tent to sleep in. We would need the tent once we reached Olympia. There were no houses there. Once the games started there would be thousands of tents in the fields around the valley of Olympia. Those who were very poor would sleep on the ground. But no one minded. Nor did Diagoras mind carrying the heavy tent. All he could think of was that soon he would be in Olympia. And there he would see the greatest athletes in Greece.

After many days of walking, we came to the final hill. The valley of Olympia lay at our feet. I told Diagoras what my father had once told me. "A poet once called this very place the fairest spot in all of Greece." I could tell Diagoras felt the same way. Before us was a land alive with beautiful flowers and heavily wooded with olive trees. Softly rolling hills lay just to the north. Snow-capped mountains rose to the east, past great open fields. Around the valley to the south and west were shining rivers.

Diagoras and I started down into the valley. The great temples of Zeus and Hera rose high above everything else. Diagoras could not take it all in. The sight was too much for him. And then we saw it—the great stadium. For hundreds of years the sight of it had

welcomed Greece's greatest athletes. And there was the *hippodrome,* the race course where the chariot races would be held.

There was so much for Diagoras to see, so many great buildings. And everywhere we looked small altars and statues of the gods dotted the fields. For Olympia was still a place of religious worship. The honor that the athletes won in the games was still less important than the honor they gave to the gods by winning.

More and more people walked into the valley. I was happy Diagoras was there to see it all. It was like being at a great party! Musicians and poets moved among the people playing and singing songs. Artists sold their paintings. Food and drinks were sold. Even animals were sold. Later they would be given as gifts to the gods. And in the middle of all this, everyone was trying to guess who would win. Men were picking the athlete they liked best — or any athlete who happened to come from their city.

My son's eyes grew wider and wider. Yes, Olympia was really something to see. But Diagoras seemed not to see just Olympia. I think he *felt* it — in his heart, in his mind, in every part of his strong young body. He tried to tell me how he felt. I put my hand on his arm and he stopped trying. He did not have to say anything. His eyes told me.

Chapter 4

The Games Begin

The next morning we awoke to the sound of horns. There were excited shouts from the crowd. This was the day of the full moon. The Olympics would begin! There would be no games on this first day, only prayers and gifts for Zeus. These would be followed by parades. Then there would be a great meal and music.

Now the athletes were leaving the great temple. There they swore to work as hard as they could. They were here to play for the glory of Zeus even before their own glory. Fair play was as important as winning itself.

The athletes moved into the stadium to meet the crowd. To one side of each young man stood his proud father. To the other side was the man who had trained the athlete for the past ten months. One by one, a leader called out the name of each athlete, his father's name, and where he came from. The crowd cheered loudly for each man.

I leaned over to Diagoras and whispered, "Some day your name will be called out in this stadium."

"And yours too, Papa," Diagoras said, smiling at me.

Diagoras wanted to walk through the stadium. He told me he just wanted to know what it felt like to stand on the playing field. But I knew what he was really after. Diagoras wanted to meet some of the athletes, to talk with them — to learn from them.

I stood at the far end of the field and watched my son move from one group of people to the next. Each athlete had a small number of men around him. Diagoras tried to hear every word they said. He stopped near one group when suddenly a hand reached out and grabbed his robe. Diagoras was picked up off his feet by the strong hand. My poor son — he was so frightened! From where I stood I could see who was lifting him. It was Aulos, a strong athlete from the city of Corinth.

Aulos was smiling now. So was Diagoras. Aulos and his father talked with Diagoras for a while and Aulos shook his hand. I thought my son's feet would leave the ground forever. He was that proud! Just as Diagoras was turning away, Aulos grabbed his arm. He

showed Diagoras the *discus* he would throw in the morning. It was a round flat stone. Aulos picked it up and held it out to Diagoras. The boy tried to hold it, but it was so heavy that he almost fell over when Aulos let go.

Diagoras had been throwing a discus for the last year or so. But the discus he used was a small metal one. Aulos had handed him the Olympic discus — 15 pounds of stone! I think this was Aulos's way of showing Diagoras that he had some muscle building to do before his turn to play would come. I saw Aulos whisper something to Diagoras before we left the stadium. Diagoras said nothing to me, so I did not ask him what Aulos had said. But I *did* wonder.

The next morning the games began. We got to the main stadium early — in time to see discus and javelin throwing contests. These Olympic athletes sent the discus sailing as if the heavy stone weighed nothing. The *javelins* were long and shaped like spears. We could hardly see them as they flew across the stadium.

Diagoras was excited with the throwing games. But soon he pulled me to move faster to the hippodrome. He could not wait to see the great chariot race. Forty chariots would be in today's race — each to be pulled by four horses. Even though the track was large, it did not seem big enough for 40 drivers and 160 horses.

With a crack of the whip, the race was on. The sound of hoof beats and men's cries filled the air. With so many chariots on the field, there was not enough room to make the first turn around the post. The chariot wheels skidded wildly. A driver tumbled into the path of the horses coming from behind. I pulled Diagoras to me and held him close. I know you will tell me the boy was already 13 years old. But is anyone ever old enough to see such things as this?

At the far post a driver tried rounding the turn sharply. His horses could not make it. The chariot turned over right in front of another chariot. The crashes came one after another. The rushing horses could not move out of the way in time. From all over the field there were cries of pain. Men and animals were being pounded by the oncoming chariots.

There would be very few chariots and drivers left by the end of this race. Diagoras looked up at me. In his eyes there was a look more of sadness than fright. "Papa," he suddenly said, "why do these men risk their lives to win? Do they love racing so much? Is the olive branch so important to them?"

"No, Diagoras. It is not the love of racing. And it is not the olive branch they are after. As a matter of fact, the winning driver does not even get the olive branch. That prize goes to the owner of the chariot. These drivers are here because they love *money*. They are

paid to race by the owners of the chariots. Some rich men have six chariots in this race. But they only have to pay the drivers that finish the whole race!"

By the end of the race only three chariots were left. Diagoras did not even want to stay to see the winner. He was very quiet the rest of the day and into the evening. We ate in silence. I tried to think of something to say. Finally, when Diagoras was ready for bed, I asked him what Aulos had whispered to him that first day. The boy never answered. Perhaps he was asleep.

All week long Diagoras and I watched the great Olympic games. We saw the high jumpers, the broad jumpers, the horseback riders, the runners, and the wrestlers. Diagoras knew he was watching the greatest athletes in all of Greece — perhaps the whole world. They were so strong, fast, and able. To Diagoras they were more than human. And the more he saw them the more he longed to be one of them.

Diagoras was happiest with the wrestling and boxing games. They were held on the grass in front of the altar of Zeus. The boxers wore pieces of leather around their hands. Some had bits of metal or nails stuck into these leather straps. It was a very rough sport. There were no rounds and no judges to decide who won. The fight ended only when one of the men raised a finger as a sign that he had had enough. Diagoras thought that

the strongest man would always win at boxing. But I told him that a quick mind was just as important to the Greek boxer.

I told Diagoras the story of an Olympic boxer named Eurydamas. Once Eurydamas had all his teeth knocked out by the man he was fighting. But he would not show the other boxer he was hurt. Instead he *swallowed* the teeth. The other man was so tired he was about to drop. He could not think of any way to beat Eurydamas. So he just gave up. Eurydamas was toothless — but he was the winner!

The week passed far too quickly for everyone. But we all looked forward to the final day. That was the day of the greatest of all Olympic games. It was the day of the *Pentathlon.* This was not one game, but a group of five different ones. There was running, jumping, wrestling, discus throwing, and javelin throwing. All the other Olympic games were held to find the best athlete in each sport. But the winner of the Pentathlon would be the greatest *all-around* athlete in Greece. He would have to make the best showing in all five contests.

All day long we watched the final games. We were too excited to even think about eating. Only the greatest of the great had been found good enough for the Pentathlon. And when it was over, Diagoras could not have been happier. Not that the winner was even from our city of Arcadia. He was from Corinth. It was Aulos, the young man who had been so nice to Diagoras on his first visit to Olympia.

Aulos walked up to the judges. He was given the special olive branch. The crowd was so loud we had to cover our ears. His father stood nearby, crying with pride and joy. And why not? His son had just been raised almost as high as the gods themselves.

I looked at Diagoras. I really think he saw the two of us standing where Aulos and his father now stood. And

then Diagoras told me what Aulos had whispered to him that first day. He told my son that the great god Zeus had told him two things that day. One was that he, Aulos, would win the Pentathlon. The other was that a young boy from Arcadia would be the next winner.

The next morning we started our long trip back to Arcadia. But when I looked at Diagoras I knew nothing would ever be the same for him again. Diagoras had come to Olympia filled with wonder. He was returning home with a dream that he had to make come true.

Chapter 5

Diagoras Trains for the Games

By the time Diagoras was 16, he had the body of a man. His arms and legs were strong. And he was well known as an athlete. Not only in Arcadia but in nearby city-states as well. It was three years since he had seen his first games at Olympia.

One morning the sound of horns came from the wall at the edge of the city. We all ran to see what was happening. There were men on horses dressed in bright colors and carrying flags. They were going from city to city to tell all Greeks something very important.

The Olympic games will be held next summer at the August full moon. Any man in this city who wishes to enter the games must go to the city of Elis immediately. There he will be tested. Good athletes will stay ten months to train.

The crowd was busy talking. I watched Diagoras turn red as people pointed fingers at him.

"Diagoras is ready for the Olympic games. He is the greatest athlete in Arcadia and all the other cities around here. His father should take him to Elis." That was pretty much what people were saying.

I asked Diagoras that very day if he wanted to try for the Olympic games. "I am willing to try, Papa," he told me. "But am I good enough?" I did not answer him. I knew he could see the answer in my eyes. My son was a man now. We did not need so many words together.

So we set out together once again. Elis was very close to Olympia. It was the city that really ran the Olympic games. Every Olympic judge was from Elis. And there was a hall for training the Olympic athletes.

In Elis Diagoras met hundreds of other young men who hoped, as he hoped, to be in the next Olympics. They would have to pass a test for each Olympic sport. It took weeks. Diagoras and the others could hardly keep their eyes open at evening meals. But at last the tests were all over. Now the young men waited to hear from the judges.

The gods smiled upon my son! Diagoras would play in the Olympic games! Oh, I knew it. I had known this would happen ever since the boy was nine. But that did not make me any less proud. I cried and so did Diagoras. There we were — in the middle of all those fathers and sons — crying with joy.

But as proud and happy as Diagoras was, we both knew what the next ten months would be like. He would work night and day, harder than ever before. He would have to train his whole body for the Olympic games. I asked myself what any father asks himself. Will he be able to get through it? I think I knew the answer, even then.

Diagoras and I said goodbye. I would return to Arcadia alone. The next time I would see my son would be in the valley of Olympia. If you have a father, or even a good friend, maybe you will know what it was like for us to say goodbye that day.

Later, Diagoras told me he had no idea what he was getting into. The next ten months were like a bad dream. Every day he would run and jump and wrestle and exercise. Every part of his body hurt. At night he would ask the gods for rest. But he knew there was little time to rest. If he was to win the olive branch, he had to go on.

And don't think that we Greeks took our children out of school for the Olympics. During each long day Diagoras pushed his body. And each evening he pushed his *mind*. Along with the others he learned history, science — everything that schoolboys learned. Diagoras soon found that the Olympics winner was the Greek idea of a perfect man. *A good mind in a good body*.

Many of the young men could not stand so much hard work. They gave up and went home. But Diagoras would not stop. He would win the Pentathlon for the glory of Zeus. He would not fail Arcadia or his father.

Chapter 6

The Dream Comes True

Summer came. The August full moon would soon be here. From everywhere in Greece people moved toward the valley of Olympia. It was the time of the great games. I had not seen Diagoras for almost a year.

Diagoras looked two heads taller to me. He had grown so! When he asked me about my trip from Arcadia my face turned red. How could I tell Diagoras the truth? I was hardly ever alone. Everyone I met along the way I told about my son. When they heard he was taking part in the great games they made me sit down with them, eat their food, and ride their horses.

But the best was yet to come for me. As the father of an Olympic player I was given a wonderful tent, food, and gifts of all kinds. Diagoras was very happy about it all. He knew how hard it had been to work all year without him.

"What games have they asked you to try, Diagoras?"

"The Pentathlon, Father."

The word seemed so easy for him I thought I had not heard right. I asked him again. He laughed and told me I had indeed heard him the first time. "The pen ... the pentath ... the *pentathlon!*" I was shouting the word. I could not believe it. Diagoras could only laugh. And then I started laughing too — so hard I could not stop for a long time.

And now the great morning arrived at last. The judges called, "Diagoras, son of Pindar, from Arcadia." The crowd cheered, and Diagoras stepped forward. The sound of the cheering was like music to me. But would they still be cheering for him at the end of the week? That, of course, I could not know. And I did not really care. Four years ago Diagoras had sat and watched these games. This week he would be playing them. That was enough for me. I only hoped it would be enough for Diagoras.

The rest of the story you know. I can still hear the cheers of the crowd. The sound was like thunder. The judge had just said the words that the athlete Aulos had whispered to my son four years before: *Diagoras, son of Pindar, from the city of Arcadia has won the Pentathlon.*

The ancient Greek Olympics went on for another
800 years after the time of Diagoras. Then, nearly 12
centuries later, Greece was under Roman rule. In the
year 393 A.D. the Roman emperor put an end to the
Olympics. He said that they were played for Greek,
not Roman, gods. And so the great event that had been
born from a feeling brotherhood ended in religious
hatred.

Fifteen hundred years went by and most of the
world forgot there had been any such thing as the
Olympics. But at least one man remembered. In the
late 1800s a Frenchman became interested in the
ancient Olympic games. His name was Baron Pierre
de Coubertin. He had read every history book he
could find about ancient Greece.

Baron de Coubertin believed the world could learn a lot about friendship and fair play from the ancient Greeks and their Olympic games. He wondered what would happen if athletes from all over the *world* came to play the Olympic games every four years. Perhaps, he thought, it would bring the people of the world closer together. Might it even end wars between countries?

In 1894 de Coubertin set up a meeting of people from 12 different nations. They agreed to give his idea a chance.

Two years later, in 1896, the first games of the modern Olympics were held in Athens, Greece. It seemed right that Greece should be the place to start the games. A great new marble Olympic stadium was built in Athens. And the king of Greece was there to welcome all the athletes who had come to his country.

But while the Olympic games have grown over the years, they have still not kept the promise of ending wars. The games have been held every four years since 1896 except for the years during the two world wars. The number of countries taking part in the Olympics has grown to more than 100. Most important, women have been allowed to play in the games since 1912. Their games are now every bit as popular as those of the male Olympic athletes.

Today the Olympic games are more important than ever before. Hundreds of thousands of people go to the city where they are being held just to see the games. Athletes who love sport for its own sake train for years to be good enough for the Olympics.

Baron de Coubertin wrote these words in the 19th century, but they might have been spoken by Diagoras or his father 25 centuries ago:

The most important thing in the Olympic games is not to win but to take part. Just as the most important thing in life is not the winning but the struggle. The main thing is not to have won but to have fought well.